BROADMAN
CHURCH SUPPLIES

Scripture from KJV
840154558060

Celebrate The Child

FOR UNTO US A CHILD IS BORN, UNTO US A SON IS GIVEN: AND THE GOVERNMENT SHALL BE UPON HIS SHOULDER: AND HIS NAME SHALL BE CALLED WONDERFUL, COUNSELLOR, THE MIGHTY GOD, THE EVERLASTING FATHER, THE PRINCE OF PEACE.

ISAIAH 9:6

CELEBRATE THE CHILD

FOR UNTO US A CHILD IS BORN,
UNTO US A SON IS GIVEN: AND THE
GOVERNMENT SHALL BE UPON HIS
SHOULDER: AND HIS NAME SHALL BE
CALLED WONDERFUL, COUNSELLOR, THE
MIGHTY GOD, THE EVERLASTING FATHER,
THE PRINCE OF PEACE.

ISAIAH 9:6

BROADMAN
CHURCH SUPPLIES

Scripture from KJV
840154558060

Celebrate The Child

FOR UNTO US A CHILD IS BORN, UNTO US A SON IS GIVEN: AND THE GOVERNMENT SHALL BE UPON HIS SHOULDER: AND HIS NAME SHALL BE CALLED WONDERFUL, COUNSELLOR, THE MIGHTY GOD, THE EVERLASTING FATHER, THE PRINCE OF PEACE.

ISAIAH 9:6

BROADMAN
CHURCH SUPPLIES

Scripture from KJV
840154558060

Celebrate The Child

FOR UNTO US A CHILD IS BORN,
UNTO US A SON IS GIVEN: AND THE
GOVERNMENT SHALL BE UPON HIS
SHOULDER: AND HIS NAME SHALL BE
CALLED WONDERFUL, COUNSELLOR, THE
MIGHTY GOD, THE EVERLASTING FATHER,
THE PRINCE OF PEACE.

ISAIAH 9:6

BROADMAN
CHURCH SUPPLIES

Scripture from KJV
840154558060

BROADMAN CHURCH SUPPLIES

Scripture from KJV
840154558060

Celebrate The Child

FOR UNTO US A CHILD IS BORN, UNTO US A SON IS GIVEN: AND THE GOVERNMENT SHALL BE UPON HIS SHOULDER: AND HIS NAME SHALL BE CALLED WONDERFUL, COUNSELLOR, THE MIGHTY GOD, THE EVERLASTING FATHER, THE PRINCE OF PEACE.

ISAIAH 9:6

BROADMAN CHURCH SUPPLIES

Scripture from KJV
840154558060

CELEBRATE THE CHILD

FOR UNTO US A CHILD IS BORN,
UNTO US A SON IS GIVEN: AND THE
GOVERNMENT SHALL BE UPON HIS
SHOULDER: AND HIS NAME SHALL BE
CALLED WONDERFUL, COUNSELLOR, THE
MIGHTY GOD, THE EVERLASTING FATHER,
THE PRINCE OF PEACE.

ISAIAH 9:6

BROADMAN
CHURCH SUPPLIES

Scripture from KJV
840154558060

BROADMAN
CHURCH SUPPLIES

Scripture from KJV
840154558060

BROADMAN CHURCH SUPPLIES

Scripture from KJV
840154558060

CELEBRATE THE CHILD

FOR UNTO US A CHILD IS BORN, UNTO US A SON IS GIVEN: AND THE GOVERNMENT SHALL BE UPON HIS SHOULDER: AND HIS NAME SHALL BE CALLED WONDERFUL, COUNSELLOR, THE MIGHTY GOD, THE EVERLASTING FATHER, THE PRINCE OF PEACE.

ISAIAH 9:6

Celebrate The Child

FOR UNTO US A CHILD IS BORN, UNTO US A SON IS GIVEN: AND THE GOVERNMENT SHALL BE UPON HIS SHOULDER: AND HIS NAME SHALL BE CALLED WONDERFUL, COUNSELLOR, THE MIGHTY GOD, THE EVERLASTING FATHER, THE PRINCE OF PEACE.

ISAIAH 9:6

BROADMAN
CHURCH SUPPLIES

Scripture from KJV
840154558060

BROADMAN
CHURCH SUPPLIES

Scripture from KJV
840154558060

BROADMAN
CHURCH SUPPLIES

Scripture from KJV
840154558060

Celebrate The Child

FOR UNTO US A CHILD IS BORN, UNTO US A SON IS GIVEN: AND THE GOVERNMENT SHALL BE UPON HIS SHOULDER: AND HIS NAME SHALL BE CALLED WONDERFUL, COUNSELLOR, THE MIGHTY GOD, THE EVERLASTING FATHER, THE PRINCE OF PEACE.

ISAIAH 9:6

BROADMAN
CHURCH SUPPLIES

Scripture from KJV
840154558060

BROADMAN CHURCH SUPPLIES

Scripture from KJV
840154558060

CELEBRATE THE CHILD

FOR UNTO US A CHILD IS BORN, UNTO US A SON IS GIVEN: AND THE GOVERNMENT SHALL BE UPON HIS SHOULDER: AND HIS NAME SHALL BE CALLED WONDERFUL, COUNSELLOR, THE MIGHTY GOD, THE EVERLASTING FATHER, THE PRINCE OF PEACE.

ISAIAH 9:6

BROADMAN
CHURCH SUPPLIES

Scripture from KJV
840154558060

BROADMAN CHURCH SUPPLIES

Scripture from KJV
840154558060

BROADMAN
CHURCH SUPPLIES

Scripture from KJV
840154558060

BROADMAN CHURCH SUPPLIES

Scripture from KJV
840154558060

Celebrate The Child

FOR UNTO US A CHILD IS BORN, UNTO US A SON IS GIVEN: AND THE GOVERNMENT SHALL BE UPON HIS SHOULDER: AND HIS NAME SHALL BE CALLED WONDERFUL, COUNSELLOR, THE MIGHTY GOD, THE EVERLASTING FATHER, THE PRINCE OF PEACE.

ISAIAH 9:6

BROADMAN CHURCH SUPPLIES

Scripture from KJV
840154558060

Celebrate the Child

FOR UNTO US A CHILD IS BORN, UNTO US A SON IS GIVEN: AND THE GOVERNMENT SHALL BE UPON HIS SHOULDER: AND HIS NAME SHALL BE CALLED WONDERFUL, COUNSELLOR, THE MIGHTY GOD, THE EVERLASTING FATHER, THE PRINCE OF PEACE.

ISAIAH 9:6

BROADMAN CHURCH SUPPLIES

Scripture from KJV
840154558060

CELEBRATE THE CHILD

FOR UNTO US A CHILD IS BORN, UNTO US A SON IS GIVEN: AND THE GOVERNMENT SHALL BE UPON HIS SHOULDER: AND HIS NAME SHALL BE CALLED WONDERFUL, COUNSELLOR, THE MIGHTY GOD, THE EVERLASTING FATHER, THE PRINCE OF PEACE.

ISAIAH 9:6

BROADMAN CHURCH SUPPLIES

Scripture from KJV
840154558060

CELEBRATE THE CHILD

FOR UNTO US A CHILD IS BORN, UNTO US A SON IS GIVEN: AND THE GOVERNMENT SHALL BE UPON HIS SHOULDER: AND HIS NAME SHALL BE CALLED WONDERFUL, COUNSELLOR, THE MIGHTY GOD, THE EVERLASTING FATHER, THE PRINCE OF PEACE.

ISAIAH 9:6

BROADMAN CHURCH SUPPLIES

Scripture from KJV
840154558060

BROADMAN
CHURCH SUPPLIES

Scripture from KJV
840154558060

BROADMAN CHURCH SUPPLIES

Scripture from KJV
840154558060

BROADMAN
CHURCH SUPPLIES

Scripture from KJV
840154558060

CELEBRATE THE CHILD

FOR UNTO US A CHILD IS BORN, UNTO US A SON IS GIVEN: AND THE GOVERNMENT SHALL BE UPON HIS SHOULDER: AND HIS NAME SHALL BE CALLED WONDERFUL, COUNSELLOR, THE MIGHTY GOD, THE EVERLASTING FATHER, THE PRINCE OF PEACE.

ISAIAH 9:6

BROADMAN CHURCH SUPPLIES

Scripture from KJV
840154558060

BROADMAN CHURCH SUPPLIES

Scripture from KJV
840154558060

BROADMAN
CHURCH SUPPLIES

Scripture from KJV
840154558060

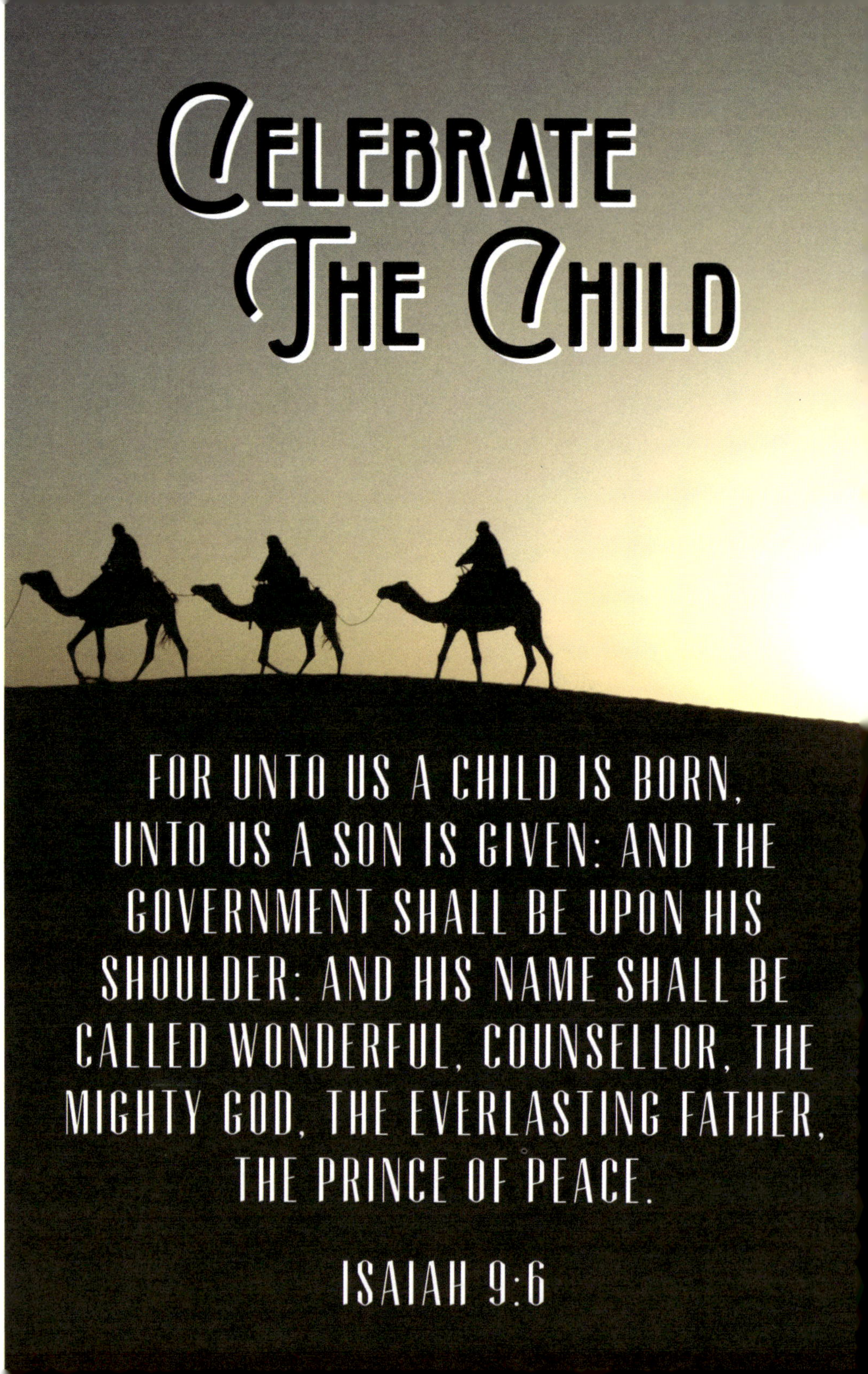

Celebrate The Child

FOR UNTO US A CHILD IS BORN, UNTO US A SON IS GIVEN: AND THE GOVERNMENT SHALL BE UPON HIS SHOULDER: AND HIS NAME SHALL BE CALLED WONDERFUL, COUNSELLOR, THE MIGHTY GOD, THE EVERLASTING FATHER, THE PRINCE OF PEACE.

ISAIAH 9:6

BROADMAN
CHURCH SUPPLIES

Scripture from KJV
840154558060

BROADMAN
CHURCH SUPPLIES

Scripture from KJV
840154558060

Celebrate The Child

FOR UNTO US A CHILD IS BORN, UNTO US A SON IS GIVEN: AND THE GOVERNMENT SHALL BE UPON HIS SHOULDER: AND HIS NAME SHALL BE CALLED WONDERFUL, COUNSELLOR, THE MIGHTY GOD, THE EVERLASTING FATHER, THE PRINCE OF PEACE.

ISAIAH 9:6

CELEBRATE THE CHILD

FOR UNTO US A CHILD IS BORN,
UNTO US A SON IS GIVEN: AND THE
GOVERNMENT SHALL BE UPON HIS
SHOULDER: AND HIS NAME SHALL BE
CALLED WONDERFUL, COUNSELLOR, THE
MIGHTY GOD, THE EVERLASTING FATHER,
THE PRINCE OF PEACE.

ISAIAH 9:6

BROADMAN CHURCH SUPPLIES

Scripture from KJV
840154558060

Celebrate The Child

FOR UNTO US A CHILD IS BORN, UNTO US A SON IS GIVEN: AND THE GOVERNMENT SHALL BE UPON HIS SHOULDER: AND HIS NAME SHALL BE CALLED WONDERFUL, COUNSELLOR, THE MIGHTY GOD, THE EVERLASTING FATHER, THE PRINCE OF PEACE.

ISAIAH 9:6

BROADMAN
CHURCH SUPPLIES

Scripture from KJV
840154558060

CELEBRATE THE CHILD

FOR UNTO US A CHILD IS BORN, UNTO US A SON IS GIVEN: AND THE GOVERNMENT SHALL BE UPON HIS SHOULDER: AND HIS NAME SHALL BE CALLED WONDERFUL, COUNSELLOR, THE MIGHTY GOD, THE EVERLASTING FATHER, THE PRINCE OF PEACE.

ISAIAH 9:6

BROADMAN
CHURCH SUPPLIES

Scripture from KJV
840154558060

BROADMAN
CHURCH SUPPLIES

Scripture from KJV
840154558060

BROADMAN
CHURCH SUPPLIES

Scripture from KJV
840154558060

CELEBRATE THE CHILD

FOR UNTO US A CHILD IS BORN, UNTO US A SON IS GIVEN: AND THE GOVERNMENT SHALL BE UPON HIS SHOULDER: AND HIS NAME SHALL BE CALLED WONDERFUL, COUNSELLOR, THE MIGHTY GOD, THE EVERLASTING FATHER, THE PRINCE OF PEACE.

ISAIAH 9:6

Celebrate The Child

FOR UNTO US A CHILD IS BORN,
UNTO US A SON IS GIVEN: AND THE
GOVERNMENT SHALL BE UPON HIS
SHOULDER: AND HIS NAME SHALL BE
CALLED WONDERFUL, COUNSELLOR, THE
MIGHTY GOD, THE EVERLASTING FATHER,
THE PRINCE OF PEACE.

ISAIAH 9:6

BROADMAN CHURCH SUPPLIES

Scripture from KJV
840154558060

BROADMAN
CHURCH SUPPLIES

Scripture from KJV
840154558060

CELEBRATE THE CHILD

FOR UNTO US A CHILD IS BORN, UNTO US A SON IS GIVEN: AND THE GOVERNMENT SHALL BE UPON HIS SHOULDER: AND HIS NAME SHALL BE CALLED WONDERFUL, COUNSELLOR, THE MIGHTY GOD, THE EVERLASTING FATHER, THE PRINCE OF PEACE.

ISAIAH 9:6

BROADMAN
CHURCH SUPPLIES

Scripture from KJV
840154558060

CELEBRATE THE CHILD

FOR UNTO US A CHILD IS BORN, UNTO US A SON IS GIVEN: AND THE GOVERNMENT SHALL BE UPON HIS SHOULDER: AND HIS NAME SHALL BE CALLED WONDERFUL, COUNSELLOR, THE MIGHTY GOD, THE EVERLASTING FATHER, THE PRINCE OF PEACE.

ISAIAH 9:6

BROADMAN CHURCH SUPPLIES

Scripture from KJV
840154558060

CELEBRATE THE CHILD

FOR UNTO US A CHILD IS BORN, UNTO US A SON IS GIVEN: AND THE GOVERNMENT SHALL BE UPON HIS SHOULDER: AND HIS NAME SHALL BE CALLED WONDERFUL, COUNSELLOR, THE MIGHTY GOD, THE EVERLASTING FATHER, THE PRINCE OF PEACE.

ISAIAH 9:6

BROADMAN CHURCH SUPPLIES

Scripture from KJV
840154558060

BROADMAN
CHURCH SUPPLIES

Scripture from KJV
840154558060

Celebrate The Child

FOR UNTO US A CHILD IS BORN,
UNTO US A SON IS GIVEN: AND THE
GOVERNMENT SHALL BE UPON HIS
SHOULDER: AND HIS NAME SHALL BE
CALLED WONDERFUL, COUNSELLOR, THE
MIGHTY GOD, THE EVERLASTING FATHER,
THE PRINCE OF PEACE.

ISAIAH 9:6

BROADMAN
CHURCH SUPPLIES

Scripture from KJV
840154558060

BROADMAN CHURCH SUPPLIES

Scripture from KJV
840154558060

BROADMAN
CHURCH SUPPLIES

Scripture from KJV
840154558060

BROADMAN CHURCH SUPPLIES

Scripture from KJV
840154558060

BROADMAN CHURCH SUPPLIES

Scripture from KJV
840154558060

Celebrate The Child

FOR UNTO US A CHILD IS BORN, UNTO US A SON IS GIVEN: AND THE GOVERNMENT SHALL BE UPON HIS SHOULDER: AND HIS NAME SHALL BE CALLED WONDERFUL, COUNSELLOR, THE MIGHTY GOD, THE EVERLASTING FATHER, THE PRINCE OF PEACE.

ISAIAH 9:6

BROADMAN
CHURCH SUPPLIES

Scripture from KJV
840154558060

BROADMAN
CHURCH SUPPLIES

Scripture from KJV
840154558060

BROADMAN CHURCH SUPPLIES

Scripture from KJV
840154558060

BROADMAN
CHURCH SUPPLIES

Scripture from KJV
840154558060

BROADMAN
CHURCH SUPPLIES

Scripture from KJV
840154558060

BROADMAN CHURCH SUPPLIES

Scripture from KJV
840154558060

CELEBRATE THE CHILD

FOR UNTO US A CHILD IS BORN, UNTO US A SON IS GIVEN: AND THE GOVERNMENT SHALL BE UPON HIS SHOULDER: AND HIS NAME SHALL BE CALLED WONDERFUL, COUNSELLOR, THE MIGHTY GOD, THE EVERLASTING FATHER, THE PRINCE OF PEACE.

ISAIAH 9:6

Celebrate The Child

FOR UNTO US A CHILD IS BORN, UNTO US A SON IS GIVEN: AND THE GOVERNMENT SHALL BE UPON HIS SHOULDER: AND HIS NAME SHALL BE CALLED WONDERFUL, COUNSELLOR, THE MIGHTY GOD, THE EVERLASTING FATHER, THE PRINCE OF PEACE.

ISAIAH 9:6

BROADMAN
CHURCH SUPPLIES

Scripture from KJV
840154558060

BROADMAN
CHURCH SUPPLIES

Scripture from KJV
840154558060

CELEBRATE THE CHILD

FOR UNTO US A CHILD IS BORN, UNTO US A SON IS GIVEN: AND THE GOVERNMENT SHALL BE UPON HIS SHOULDER: AND HIS NAME SHALL BE CALLED WONDERFUL, COUNSELLOR, THE MIGHTY GOD, THE EVERLASTING FATHER, THE PRINCE OF PEACE.

ISAIAH 9:6

BROADMAN CHURCH SUPPLIES

Scripture from KJV
840154558060

BROADMAN CHURCH SUPPLIES

Scripture from KJV
840154558060

CELEBRATE THE CHILD

FOR UNTO US A CHILD IS BORN, UNTO US A SON IS GIVEN: AND THE GOVERNMENT SHALL BE UPON HIS SHOULDER: AND HIS NAME SHALL BE CALLED WONDERFUL, COUNSELLOR, THE MIGHTY GOD, THE EVERLASTING FATHER, THE PRINCE OF PEACE.

ISAIAH 9:6

BROADMAN
CHURCH SUPPLIES

Scripture from KJV
840154558060

CELEBRATE THE CHILD

FOR UNTO US A CHILD IS BORN, UNTO US A SON IS GIVEN: AND THE GOVERNMENT SHALL BE UPON HIS SHOULDER: AND HIS NAME SHALL BE CALLED WONDERFUL, COUNSELLOR, THE MIGHTY GOD, THE EVERLASTING FATHER, THE PRINCE OF PEACE.

ISAIAH 9:6

BROADMAN CHURCH SUPPLIES

Scripture from KJV
840154558060

BROADMAN
CHURCH SUPPLIES

Scripture from KJV
840154558060

Celebrate The Child

FOR UNTO US A CHILD IS BORN,
UNTO US A SON IS GIVEN: AND THE
GOVERNMENT SHALL BE UPON HIS
SHOULDER: AND HIS NAME SHALL BE
CALLED WONDERFUL, COUNSELLOR, THE
MIGHTY GOD, THE EVERLASTING FATHER,
THE PRINCE OF PEACE.

ISAIAH 9:6

CELEBRATE THE CHILD

FOR UNTO US A CHILD IS BORN, UNTO US A SON IS GIVEN: AND THE GOVERNMENT SHALL BE UPON HIS SHOULDER: AND HIS NAME SHALL BE CALLED WONDERFUL, COUNSELLOR, THE MIGHTY GOD, THE EVERLASTING FATHER, THE PRINCE OF PEACE.

ISAIAH 9:6

BROADMAN
CHURCH SUPPLIES

Scripture from KJV
840154558060

BROADMAN CHURCH SUPPLIES

Scripture from KJV
840154558060

CELEBRATE THE CHILD

FOR UNTO US A CHILD IS BORN, UNTO US A SON IS GIVEN: AND THE GOVERNMENT SHALL BE UPON HIS SHOULDER: AND HIS NAME SHALL BE CALLED WONDERFUL, COUNSELLOR, THE MIGHTY GOD, THE EVERLASTING FATHER, THE PRINCE OF PEACE.

ISAIAH 9:6

BROADMAN
CHURCH SUPPLIES

Scripture from KJV
840154558060

BROADMAN CHURCH SUPPLIES

Scripture from KJV
840154558060

CELEBRATE THE CHILD

FOR UNTO US A CHILD IS BORN, UNTO US A SON IS GIVEN: AND THE GOVERNMENT SHALL BE UPON HIS SHOULDER: AND HIS NAME SHALL BE CALLED WONDERFUL, COUNSELLOR, THE MIGHTY GOD, THE EVERLASTING FATHER, THE PRINCE OF PEACE.

ISAIAH 9:6

BROADMAN CHURCH SUPPLIES

Scripture from KJV
840154558060

CELEBRATE THE CHILD

FOR UNTO US A CHILD IS BORN, UNTO US A SON IS GIVEN: AND THE GOVERNMENT SHALL BE UPON HIS SHOULDER: AND HIS NAME SHALL BE CALLED WONDERFUL, COUNSELLOR, THE MIGHTY GOD, THE EVERLASTING FATHER, THE PRINCE OF PEACE.

ISAIAH 9:6

BROADMAN
CHURCH SUPPLIES

Scripture from KJV
840154558060

CELEBRATE THE CHILD

FOR UNTO US A CHILD IS BORN, UNTO US A SON IS GIVEN: AND THE GOVERNMENT SHALL BE UPON HIS SHOULDER: AND HIS NAME SHALL BE CALLED WONDERFUL, COUNSELLOR, THE MIGHTY GOD, THE EVERLASTING FATHER, THE PRINCE OF PEACE.

ISAIAH 9:6

BROADMAN CHURCH SUPPLIES

Scripture from KJV
840154558060

CELEBRATE THE CHILD

FOR UNTO US A CHILD IS BORN,
UNTO US A SON IS GIVEN: AND THE
GOVERNMENT SHALL BE UPON HIS
SHOULDER: AND HIS NAME SHALL BE
CALLED WONDERFUL, COUNSELLOR, THE
MIGHTY GOD, THE EVERLASTING FATHER,
THE PRINCE OF PEACE.

ISAIAH 9:6

BROADMAN CHURCH SUPPLIES

Scripture from KJV
840154558060

BROADMAN
CHURCH SUPPLIES

Scripture from KJV
840154558060

BROADMAN
CHURCH SUPPLIES

Scripture from KJV
840154558060

CELEBRATE THE CHILD

FOR UNTO US A CHILD IS BORN,
UNTO US A SON IS GIVEN: AND THE
GOVERNMENT SHALL BE UPON HIS
SHOULDER: AND HIS NAME SHALL BE
CALLED WONDERFUL, COUNSELLOR, THE
MIGHTY GOD, THE EVERLASTING FATHER,
THE PRINCE OF PEACE.

ISAIAH 9:6

BROADMAN
CHURCH SUPPLIES

Scripture from KJV
840154558060

CELEBRATE THE CHILD

FOR UNTO US A CHILD IS BORN, UNTO US A SON IS GIVEN: AND THE GOVERNMENT SHALL BE UPON HIS SHOULDER: AND HIS NAME SHALL BE CALLED WONDERFUL, COUNSELLOR, THE MIGHTY GOD, THE EVERLASTING FATHER, THE PRINCE OF PEACE.

ISAIAH 9:6

BROADMAN
CHURCH SUPPLIES

Scripture from KJV
840154558060

BROADMAN
CHURCH SUPPLIES

Scripture from KJV
840154558060

CELEBRATE THE CHILD

FOR UNTO US A CHILD IS BORN, UNTO US A SON IS GIVEN: AND THE GOVERNMENT SHALL BE UPON HIS SHOULDER: AND HIS NAME SHALL BE CALLED WONDERFUL, COUNSELLOR, THE MIGHTY GOD, THE EVERLASTING FATHER, THE PRINCE OF PEACE.

ISAIAH 9:6

BROADMAN CHURCH SUPPLIES

Scripture from KJV
840154558060

BROADMAN
CHURCH SUPPLIES

Scripture from KJV
840154558060

BROADMAN
CHURCH SUPPLIES

Scripture from KJV
840154558060

BROADMAN CHURCH SUPPLIES

Scripture from KJV

840154558060

BROADMAN CHURCH SUPPLIES

Scripture from KJV
840154558060

CELEBRATE THE CHILD

FOR UNTO US A CHILD IS BORN,
UNTO US A SON IS GIVEN: AND THE
GOVERNMENT SHALL BE UPON HIS
SHOULDER: AND HIS NAME SHALL BE
CALLED WONDERFUL, COUNSELLOR, THE
MIGHTY GOD, THE EVERLASTING FATHER,
THE PRINCE OF PEACE.

ISAIAH 9:6

BROADMAN CHURCH SUPPLIES

Scripture from KJV
840154558060

BROADMAN CHURCH SUPPLIES

Scripture from KJV
840154558060

BROADMAN
CHURCH SUPPLIES

Scripture from KJV
840154558060

BROADMAN
CHURCH SUPPLIES

Scripture from KJV
840154558060

BROADMAN
CHURCH SUPPLIES

Scripture from KJV
840154558060

Celebrate The Child

FOR UNTO US A CHILD IS BORN, UNTO US A SON IS GIVEN: AND THE GOVERNMENT SHALL BE UPON HIS SHOULDER: AND HIS NAME SHALL BE CALLED WONDERFUL, COUNSELLOR, THE MIGHTY GOD, THE EVERLASTING FATHER, THE PRINCE OF PEACE.

ISAIAH 9:6

BROADMAN CHURCH SUPPLIES

Scripture from KJV
840154558060

CELEBRATE THE CHILD

FOR UNTO US A CHILD IS BORN,
UNTO US A SON IS GIVEN: AND THE GOVERNMENT SHALL BE UPON HIS SHOULDER: AND HIS NAME SHALL BE CALLED WONDERFUL, COUNSELLOR, THE MIGHTY GOD, THE EVERLASTING FATHER, THE PRINCE OF PEACE.

ISAIAH 9:6

BROADMAN CHURCH SUPPLIES

Scripture from KJV
840154558060

Celebrate The Child

FOR UNTO US A CHILD IS BORN, UNTO US A SON IS GIVEN: AND THE GOVERNMENT SHALL BE UPON HIS SHOULDER: AND HIS NAME SHALL BE CALLED WONDERFUL, COUNSELLOR, THE MIGHTY GOD, THE EVERLASTING FATHER, THE PRINCE OF PEACE.

ISAIAH 9:6

BROADMAN CHURCH SUPPLIES

Scripture from KJV
840154558060

CELEBRATE THE CHILD

FOR UNTO US A CHILD IS BORN, UNTO US A SON IS GIVEN: AND THE GOVERNMENT SHALL BE UPON HIS SHOULDER: AND HIS NAME SHALL BE CALLED WONDERFUL, COUNSELLOR, THE MIGHTY GOD, THE EVERLASTING FATHER, THE PRINCE OF PEACE.

ISAIAH 9:6

BROADMAN CHURCH SUPPLIES

Scripture from KJV
840154558060

CELEBRATE THE CHILD

FOR UNTO US A CHILD IS BORN, UNTO US A SON IS GIVEN: AND THE GOVERNMENT SHALL BE UPON HIS SHOULDER: AND HIS NAME SHALL BE CALLED WONDERFUL, COUNSELLOR, THE MIGHTY GOD, THE EVERLASTING FATHER, THE PRINCE OF PEACE.

ISAIAH 9:6

BROADMAN
CHURCH SUPPLIES

Scripture from KJV
840154558060

BROADMAN
CHURCH SUPPLIES

Scripture from KJV
840154558060

Celebrate The Child

FOR UNTO US A CHILD IS BORN, UNTO US A SON IS GIVEN: AND THE GOVERNMENT SHALL BE UPON HIS SHOULDER: AND HIS NAME SHALL BE CALLED WONDERFUL, COUNSELLOR, THE MIGHTY GOD, THE EVERLASTING FATHER, THE PRINCE OF PEACE.

ISAIAH 9:6

BROADMAN
CHURCH SUPPLIES

Scripture from KJV
840154558060

BROADMAN
CHURCH SUPPLIES

Scripture from KJV
840154558060

BROADMAN CHURCH SUPPLIES

Scripture from KJV
840154558060

CELEBRATE THE CHILD

FOR UNTO US A CHILD IS BORN, UNTO US A SON IS GIVEN: AND THE GOVERNMENT SHALL BE UPON HIS SHOULDER: AND HIS NAME SHALL BE CALLED WONDERFUL, COUNSELLOR, THE MIGHTY GOD, THE EVERLASTING FATHER, THE PRINCE OF PEACE.

ISAIAH 9:6

CELEBRATE THE CHILD

FOR UNTO US A CHILD IS BORN, UNTO US A SON IS GIVEN: AND THE GOVERNMENT SHALL BE UPON HIS SHOULDER: AND HIS NAME SHALL BE CALLED WONDERFUL, COUNSELLOR, THE MIGHTY GOD, THE EVERLASTING FATHER, THE PRINCE OF PEACE.

ISAIAH 9:6

BROADMAN CHURCH SUPPLIES

Scripture from KJV
840154558060

CELEBRATE THE CHILD

FOR UNTO US A CHILD IS BORN, UNTO US A SON IS GIVEN: AND THE GOVERNMENT SHALL BE UPON HIS SHOULDER: AND HIS NAME SHALL BE CALLED WONDERFUL, COUNSELLOR, THE MIGHTY GOD, THE EVERLASTING FATHER, THE PRINCE OF PEACE.

ISAIAH 9:6

BROADMAN CHURCH SUPPLIES

Scripture from KJV
840154558060

BROADMAN
CHURCH SUPPLIES

Scripture from KJV
840154558060

CELEBRATE THE CHILD

FOR UNTO US A CHILD IS BORN, UNTO US A SON IS GIVEN: AND THE GOVERNMENT SHALL BE UPON HIS SHOULDER: AND HIS NAME SHALL BE CALLED WONDERFUL, COUNSELLOR, THE MIGHTY GOD, THE EVERLASTING FATHER, THE PRINCE OF PEACE.

ISAIAH 9:6

CELEBRATE THE CHILD

FOR UNTO US A CHILD IS BORN, UNTO US A SON IS GIVEN: AND THE GOVERNMENT SHALL BE UPON HIS SHOULDER: AND HIS NAME SHALL BE CALLED WONDERFUL, COUNSELLOR, THE MIGHTY GOD, THE EVERLASTING FATHER, THE PRINCE OF PEACE.

ISAIAH 9:6

BROADMAN CHURCH SUPPLIES

Scripture from KJV
840154558060

BROADMAN
CHURCH SUPPLIES

Scripture from KJV
840154558060

Celebrate The Child

FOR UNTO US A CHILD IS BORN, UNTO US A SON IS GIVEN: AND THE GOVERNMENT SHALL BE UPON HIS SHOULDER: AND HIS NAME SHALL BE CALLED WONDERFUL, COUNSELLOR, THE MIGHTY GOD, THE EVERLASTING FATHER, THE PRINCE OF PEACE.

ISAIAH 9:6

CELEBRATE THE CHILD

FOR UNTO US A CHILD IS BORN, UNTO US A SON IS GIVEN: AND THE GOVERNMENT SHALL BE UPON HIS SHOULDER: AND HIS NAME SHALL BE CALLED WONDERFUL, COUNSELLOR, THE MIGHTY GOD, THE EVERLASTING FATHER, THE PRINCE OF PEACE.

ISAIAH 9:6

BROADMAN
CHURCH SUPPLIES

Scripture from KJV
840154558060

BROADMAN
CHURCH SUPPLIES

Scripture from KJV
840154558060

CELEBRATE THE CHILD

FOR UNTO US A CHILD IS BORN, UNTO US A SON IS GIVEN: AND THE GOVERNMENT SHALL BE UPON HIS SHOULDER: AND HIS NAME SHALL BE CALLED WONDERFUL, COUNSELLOR, THE MIGHTY GOD, THE EVERLASTING FATHER, THE PRINCE OF PEACE.

ISAIAH 9:6

BROADMAN
CHURCH SUPPLIES

Scripture from KJV
840154558060

Celebrate The Child

FOR UNTO US A CHILD IS BORN, UNTO US A SON IS GIVEN: AND THE GOVERNMENT SHALL BE UPON HIS SHOULDER: AND HIS NAME SHALL BE CALLED WONDERFUL, COUNSELLOR, THE MIGHTY GOD, THE EVERLASTING FATHER, THE PRINCE OF PEACE.

ISAIAH 9:6

BROADMAN CHURCH SUPPLIES

Scripture from KJV
840154558060